WILDLIFE AT RISK

ENDANGERED RHINOS

Jane Katirgis and Jan M. Czech

Enslow Publishing
101 W. 23rd Street
Suite 240
New York, NY 10011
USA

enslow.com

Published in 2016 by Enslow Publishing, LLC.
101 W. 23rd Street, Suite 240, New York, NY 10011

Library of Congress Cataloging-in-Publication Data

Katirgis, Jane, author.
 Endangered rhinos / Jane Katirgis and Jan M. Czech.
    pages cm. — (Wildlife at risk)
 Summary: "Discusses rhinos, why they are endangered and what's being done to help"— Provided by
publisher.
 Audience: Ages 11+
 Audience: Grades 7 to 8
 Includes bibliographical references and index.
 ISBN 978-0-7660-6902-2 (library binding)
 ISBN 978-0-7660-6900-8 (pbk.)
 ISBN 978-0-7660-6901-5 (6-pack)
 1. Rhinoceroses—Juvenile literature. 2. Rare mammals—Juvenile literature. I. Czech, Jan M., author. II.
Title.
 QL737.U63K38 2016
 599.66'8—dc23

                              2015010127

Printed in the United States of America

To Our Readers: We have done our best to make sure all Web site addresses in this book were active and
appropriate when we went to press. However, the author and the publisher have no control over and assume
no liability for the material available on those Web sites or on any Web sites they may link to. Any comments
or suggestions can be sent by e-mail to customerservice@enslow.com.

Portions of this book originally appeared in the book *The Rhino*.

CONTENTS

Rhinos at a Glance

Scientific Name

There are five species of rhinoceros and eleven subspecies.

Black Rhino: *Diceros bicornis*

White Rhino: *Ceratotherium simum*

Indian Rhino: *Rhinoceros unicornis*

Javan Rhino: *Rhinoceros sondaicus*

Sumatran Rhino: *Dicerorhinus sumatrensis*

Average Height

4 to 6 feet (1.2 to 1.8 m) to the shoulder

Average Weight

The five species of rhinos range from 750 pounds to 8,000 pounds (340 kg to 3,629 kg).

Life Span

In the wild, up to thirty-five years; in captivity, forty years or longer

Status

Endangered

Skin Color

Gray or brown

Teeth

Rhinos have between twenty-four and thirty-four teeth depending on the species.

Breeding Season

No particular season

Gestation Period

Varies by species but averages sixteen months

Range

Black rhinos and white rhinos are found in Africa; Javan, Indian, and Sumatran rhinos are found in Asia.

Maximum Speed

30 miles per hour (48 km per hour)

Main Threat to Survival

Humans who kill rhinos for their horns and destroy their habitat.

chapter one
THE ANCIENT RHINO

When you think of a rhinoceros, commonly called a rhino, you probably think of Africa or Asia but not Nebraska. But this large herbivore was once one of many other animals gathering around a watering hole in North America. They are long extinct in that area, but it is fascinating to think of these large beasts roaming the land with camels, horses, deer, and other animals in the area.

The rhinoceros is one of the world's most ancient animal species. It has roamed the planet for almost 50 million years. Until about 3 million years ago, rhinos were the most common land mammal in North America. There were once many more kinds of rhinos, including hornless rhinos, wooly rhinos, and the Indricotherium, which are all now extinct.

In the case of the Indricotherium, that is probably a good thing. It was the largest land mammal in the earth's history. This giant member of the rhinoceros family stood between 18 and 23 feet (5 and 7 m) tall, was 27 feet (8 m) long, and weighed about 66,000 pounds (30,000 kg). It was eight times the size of modern rhinos—as large as most houses. Other ancient rhinos looked more like horses or giraffes than their modern-day counterparts. Some scientists think that the mythical unicorn may be based on an ancient horselike one-horned rhino.

The Indricotherium, like the dinosaur and many other ancient species, no longer exists. Its modern relatives in the rhino family face the same fate—that of becoming extinct. There are now only five species and eleven subspecies of rhino, and they are found only in Africa and Asia. How could an animal that has been around for millions of years and was once so common be in danger of disappearing from the face of the earth?

Numbers on the Increase

Despite the problems of poaching, overall numbers of rhinos are steadily increasing. But human beings pose the biggest threat to the rhino population through hunting and developing the lands that once made up the rhinos' habitat. Humans have made successful attempts to build up and protect the rhino population. Yet some rhino species are now among the most critically endangered animals. The International Rhino Foundation (IRF), which supports and operates rhino conservation programs, reports that as of 2013 there were about 28,877 rhinos left in the wild. According to the IRF, there are about 20,400 white rhinos, 5,000 black rhinos, 3,333 Indian rhinos, no more than 44 Javan rhinos, and 100 Sumatran rhinos. These last two Asian rhino species are on the verge of extinction.[1]

Hunting Rhinos

The word rhinoceros comes from the Greek rhino, which means nose, and ceros, which means horn. Rhino horns are made of tightly packed hair called keratin, which is like human hair and nails. Rhinos use their horns to defend themselves against other animals. Unfortunately, it is for their horns that people hunt rhinos because those horns are highly valued in certain cultures and fetch a huge amount of money.

Poachers, or people who take or kill wild animals illegally, hunt rhinos on wildlife refuges where they are supposed to be protected. Rhinos are also hunted in the wild in their natural habitats. Rhinos often die slowly after being shot with guns or arrows. Many times, their horns are taken while they are still alive.

Although it is illegal to trade in rhino horn, poachers still supply the market with illegal rhino horn. In the 1970s and 1980s, artisans in Yemen, an Asian country at the southern tip of the Arabian peninsula, commonly used rhino horn to make handles for knives called jambiyas. Jambiyas are considered precious, like a Rolex watch, and in many families they are handed down

A hunter poses with a rhinoceros he killed around 1890.

from generation to generation. But this use of rhino horn is now responsible for fewer and fewer poaching incidents. More rhino horns are now being sold in eastern Asia to be ground up and used in medicines. The rhino horn is the most important part of the rhino to hunters, but rhino nails, hooves, blood, urine, and hide are also traded and used in medicines.

Efforts continue to protect this ancient animal, but time and tradition are both hurdles to the rhino's survival. And humans, who pose the greatest threat to the rhino's numbers, are the only ones who can now save it.

Fast Fact!

The Southern white rhino was once on the brink of extinction; there were only about 50 of them left in the wild. Today, their numbers exceed 20,000.

chapter two

A Look at Vegetarian Giants

Just like some other endangered species, including gorillas, blue whales, giant pandas, and tigers, rhinos are mammals. Rhinos are also herbivores—they eat only plants. They are either grazers, feeding mostly on grasses, or browsers, eating the leaves and branches of trees. Their lips have adapted over time to make it easier for them to graze and browse for food. Rhinos have between twenty-four and thirty-four teeth, including twelve to fourteen pairs of molars that are not sharp and are used for grinding.

Rhinos have hooves like horses and are part of the same order. They have only three toes on each hoof. A rhino's skin is different from one species to the next but is between half an inch to three quarters of an inch thick. That is about as thick as the width of your little finger.

Rhino Breeding Habits

Rhinos are not able to reproduce quickly, which also plays a part in their shrinking numbers. The rhino's gestation period, or the length of time a mother carries her young until it is born, is about sixteen months. Secondly, the male rhino, known as a bull, is not able to father a baby rhino, or calf, until he is about twelve years old. There is no set time of the year that rhinos breed or give birth. Breeding can take place any time of the year that the female, or cow, is in estrus, the period during which she can become pregnant. Female rhinos are able to reproduce at around age six and have a calf once every two or three years after that.

Even though a rhino calf nurses for about two years, it begins to eat plants when it is only a week old. While it nurses, the rhino calf is kept hidden and protected by its mother until it is strong enough to venture out on its own. While adult rhinos have no predators apart from humans, baby rhinos are in danger of being attacked by lions, hyenas, crocodiles, and tigers.

Rhino Homes

Rhinos live in the wild, in reserves, in private parks, and in captivity in zoos. Their natural habitat ranges from open grasslands, called savannas, to dense forests. Because rhinos like to drink water every day, their habitat must include a watering spot where they can not only drink but also wallow in the water and mud to cool themselves off. Rhinos can go for up to four days without water, but it is a hardship for them to do so.

Gentle Rhinos

All rhino species have a reputation for being aggressive. It is said that the black rhino will charge anything that moves. But rhinos are also easily frightened, and because their eyesight is poor, they may attack because they think an enemy is approaching. Rhinos have highly developed senses of smell and hearing, and they depend on these two senses much more than their eyesight.

Rhinos are especially gentle when it comes to birds hitching a ride. In Africa, cattle egrets can often be found riding on the backs of rhinos and other large mammals. From their perch, they have a good view of the grasshoppers and other creatures that crawl on the ground.[1] Egrets help the rhino by eating many of the bugs that live on the rhino's skin. They can also act as an early warning. If an egret sees something approaching, it will take flight, and that warns the rhino to be on the lookout.

Rhino Species

There are currently five species of rhino remaining in the world. The black rhino and the white rhino are native to Africa, although neither name adequately describes the animal's skin color, which is mostly gray. The Indian rhino, Javan rhino, and Sumatran rhino live in Asia.

The White Rhino

After the elephant, the white rhino is the largest land animal on earth. White rhinos can weigh up to 8,000 pounds (3,628 kg) and stand 6 feet (1.8 m) tall. Their name comes from the Afrikaans language spoken in South Africa. Early British settlers there misinterpreted the word weit as white.[2] *Weit*, which means wide, was used to describe the rhino's mouth.

The white rhino has two horns, one behind the other. It also has a wide, square lip and is a grazer, feeding mainly on grass. The white rhino's head is larger and heavier than the those of other rhino species. Because the white rhino grazes for food, the muscles in its neck are quite developed so it can lift its enormous head.

The International Rhino Foundation estimates that there are about 20,400 white rhinos left in Africa. This population has

An adult white rhino has two horns, as seen on the mother rhino on the right.

increased from a low of fifty animals in 1900. White rhinos are less endangered than the other four rhino species.

There are two subspecies of white rhino, and their status differs greatly. The Southern white rhino was the first rhino species to come close to extinction, but conservation efforts have boosted its population so it is now upgraded to near-threatened status. Protected on farms and reserves mainly in South Africa, its population is growing.

The Northern white rhino, on the other hand, is critically endangered. Its range used to include much of central Africa, but today it is now extinct in the wild. There are only three Northern white rhinos in the Ol Pejeta Conservancy in Kenya, Africa. Another three Northern white rhinos live in captivity in zoos in the Czech Republic and the United States. Despite efforts to save them, it is very possible that the Northern white rhino will go extinct.

The Black Rhino

The black rhino, whose name may have come from the dark soils it wallows around in, also has two horns. It is smaller than the white rhino, weighing up to 3,000 pounds (1,360 kg) and standing between 4.5 and 5.5 feet (1.4 and 1.7 m) tall. The black rhino has especially pointed prehensile lips that help it grasp the food it browses for. Both black rhinos and white rhinos have skin that hangs in folds and looks like leather with lots of knobby parts, but it is actually quite smooth and soft to the touch.

There are about 5,000 black rhinos left in the world.

Black rhinos once ranged across much of Africa but are now found in small areas in southern and eastern Africa. The black rhino population is estimated to be at 3,610, down from 65,000 in 1970.

The Indian Rhino

The Indian rhino, so called because it once lived throughout India, now lives on reserves in India and Nepal. It can weigh up to 6,000 pounds (2,721 kg) and stand about 6 feet (2 m) tall. It is the third largest land mammal, smaller only than the white rhino and the elephant. Unlike the smooth skin of the African rhinos, the most conspicuous characteristic of the Indian rhino is the deep folds in its skin. Also, the Indian rhino has only one horn.

There are about 3,333 Indian rhinos left, and theirs is a real success story. Early in the twentieth century, there were only about 200 Indian rhinos remaining. Over the years, wildlife authorities in India and Nepal have worked to protect the Indian rhino from hunters and poachers, thus allowing the rhino population a chance to grow.

Like other rhinos, the Indian rhino is generally a solitary animal. It spends long periods of time lying in water and wallowing in mud.

The Javan Rhino

The Javan rhino is the rarest of the five rhino species and also one of the most endangered since only about 44 remain. Just a single population of Javan rhinos exists, and it lives in a national park in Java, an island that is part of Indonesia. Javan rhinos weigh between 2,000 and 5,000 pounds (907 and 2,268 kg) and stand about 5 feet (1.5 m) tall. The Javan rhino has one horn and skin plates like the Indian rhino, but it is much smaller.

In 2011, the Javan Rhino became extinct in Vietnam.[3] The last remaining rhino was poached in 2010; its horns had been removed. The Javan rhino used to have a range that included India, Bangladesh, China, Myanmar, Thailand, Laos, Cambodia, Vietnam, Malaysia, and Indonesia. The species lost much of its jungle habitat during the Vietnam War. Agent Orange, a chemical agent for killing plants, was used during the war to cut down jungle growth, but it also destroyed the trees from which the rhino fed.

The Sumatran Rhino

The Sumatran rhino lives in Sumatra, an island that is part of Indonesia, and Malaysia. The Sumatran rhino population has decreased 50 percent over the past fifteen years mainly because of

The Javan rhino (shown above) is also known as the Asian lesser one-horned rhino. The Indian rhino is also referred to as the Asian greater one-horned rhino. The Javan rhino is considered "lesser" because it is smaller than the Indian rhino.

hunters. Fewer than one hundred Sumatran rhinos are alive today, but the decline has stopped thanks to the anti-poaching teams called Rhino Protection Units.

Sumatran rhinos weigh between 1,300 and 2,000 pounds (590 and 907 kg) and stand from 3 to 5 feet (under .9 to 1.5 m) tall. Like their African cousins, they have two horns. The Sumatran rhino is the only rhino species to have long hair, which is thickest when the rhino is young. Sumatran rhinos are also the only rhinos that

The number of Javan rhinos remaining in the world, which is no more than forty-four, is fewer than any of the other rhino species.

have sharp canine teeth on their lower jaw. These teeth are used for fighting.

The Sumatran rhino prefers to live in the dense forest areas of Sumatra, Myanmar, Malaysia, and Thailand. As the human population in these areas increases, the Sumatran rhino's habitat grows smaller and smaller. Another blow to the Sumatran rhino's population occurred in 2003 when all seven of the Sumatran rhinos in the Sumatra Rhino Sanctuary at Sungai Dusun in Malaysia died. Their deaths were due to an infection that was probably caused by a parasite. The same parasite causes sleeping sickness in humans.

Captive Rhinos

Rhinos can be found in captivity all over the world. Captive rhinos, moved from the wild in a process called translocation, live mainly in zoos and rhino sanctuaries. These sanctuaries can be publicly funded or paid for by private citizens. Rhinos are kept in captivity in an effort to protect them from poachers and to keep them from becoming extinct. Many sanctuaries are surrounded by electric fences to keep poachers out and are patrolled by armed guards.

Most zoos and sanctuaries have captive breeding programs to try to keep rhino populations growing. Some breeding programs are successful while others are not, and they are not without controversy. For example, the Sumatran Rhino Trust was formed, according to the group itself, to "catch enough breeding pairs of rhinos in the wild to start a viable population in captivity and thereby stem the slide toward extinction."[4] Rhino pairs were placed in zoos in the United States. The project was very expensive, and the World Wildlife Fund, for one, objected to the program and

Fast Fact!

When rhinos wallow in the mud, it cools them off. It also acts as a sunscreen and insect repellent. Once they are covered in the mud, the animal matches the color of the local soil.

said the money could have been better spent keeping the rhinos in a sanctuary in their natural habitat rather than in zoos. They may have been correct. Seven animals were placed in zoos, and soon after placement, four had died.

There have been successes, too. In 2001 at the Cincinnati Zoo, a Sumatran rhino named Emi gave birth to a calf named Andalas,

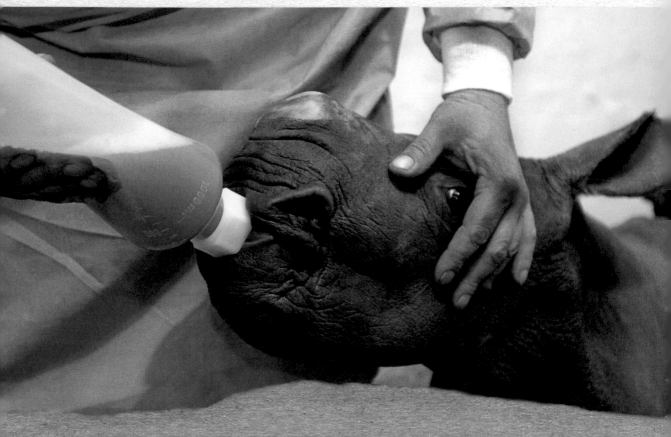

An animal keeper feeds the Budapest Zoo's newborn Southern white rhinoceros calf. Captive breeding programs help increase the number of rhinos in the world.

the first Sumatran rhino to be born and bred in captivity in 112 years. On July 30, 2004, Emi gave birth to a second calf, this time a female named Suci, an Indonesian word meaning sacred. In 2007, Emi had a third calf, named Harapan. With that birth, Emi became the first Sumatran rhino in history to produce three rhino calves in captivity.[5]

The zoo's Vice President of Conservation, Science, and Living Collections, Dr. Terry Roth, characterized the historic birth this way, "A third successful birth in just seven years clearly demonstrates how successful a well managed, captive breeding program is for this critically endangered species."[6]

In August 2004, a black rhino calf named Ajubu was born to Lembe, a first-time mother, at the San Diego Zoo's Wild Animal Park. Lembe has since had four more calves, increasing the park's total to fifteen black rhinos so far, helping the critically endangered species to survive.[7]

chapter three

THE RHINO'S PREDATOR

Habitat loss and poaching are a much bigger threat to the rhino than anything it might encounter in the wild. There is no animal predator adapted to face off with an enormous rhino and its menacing horn. Humans are the only threat to this species.

Rhino Poaching

Although international trading in rhino horns has been illegal since 1977, the practice is still a booming black market business. Poaching is the biggest threat to all rhino species. Because rhino horn and other body parts are used in traditional medicines in China and other countries in Asia, there is a thriving market for them.

Rhino Horn

Poachers hunt rhinos illegally on reserves and in their natural habitats. Most are men who live in some of the poorest countries in the world. If it were not for poaching, they would ordinarily make very little money. One rhino horn might bring them more than a year's wages earned legally.

Fast Fact!

The Indian rhino uses its teeth instead of its horns for defense. It can slash an enemy with the sharp teeth of its bottom jaw.

Between the years 2000 and 2014, the number of rhinos poached in South Africa rose from 6 to 1,215. That is one rhino every eight hours! Scientists estimate that this rate of poaching would cause rhino deaths to outnumber births by 2018. This would cause the extinction of the rhino in the near future.[1]

Poachers are usually well-equipped with weapons provided for them by the people who hire them to kill rhinos and deliver their horns. Poachers and park rangers are at war with each other over rhinos and other endangered species that live in the closely guarded game reserves. Park rangers in reserves are under orders to shoot poachers on sight. Poachers, park rangers, and others have lost their lives in the battle over rhinos.

Poachers kill rhinos with guns, spears, traps dug in the ground, and electrocution when they can find an electrical line in the rhino habitat to cut down and lay across the rhino's path. Once the rhino is downed, the poachers saw off the horns and hooves. Often, the rhino is still alive during this and dies later from its wounds.

Rhino Habitat Loss

While poaching is by far the biggest threat to the rhino, loss of habitat also plays a significant role. As human populations grow, more land is needed to support it. This often results in pushing wild animals farther and farther into their wild habitat, which often creates a compacted population. Rhinos, as grazers and browsers, require a large territory in which to roam and find food. Logging—land being cleared for large farms that produce oil palm, wood pulp, coffee, rubber, cashews, and cocoa—and people looking for land on which to settle force rhinos into smaller and smaller habitats.

The rhino has also been forced to share its habitat with people for other reasons. Civil wars in some African and Asian countries have forced many people from their homes. Some of those refugees have sought asylum in wildlife sanctuaries. Once there, the human population takes natural resources, such as water and trees, that they use for firewood and shelter. The wild animals also need these materials to survive.

As humans move into rhino territory, more and more habitat is destroyed. Not only are trees disappearing in some rhino habitats, but grass is also disappearing. Traditional nomadic herding practices that moved cattle to new pastures and prevented over-grazing have changed. Now due to economic and population demands, cattle are raised in just one place, which has a devastating effect on the savanna's ecosystem.[2] Cattle are grazers, just as some rhinos are, and as they eat the rhinos' food supply, rhinos are forced to look elsewhere. As ecosystems are destroyed, so is the rhino population.

Deforestation is a significant threat to the endangered rhino populations.

chapter four
A Plan for Rhinos

One hundred years can make quite a difference. When the 1900s began, the wild rhino population was close to one million animals. A century later, only about sixteen thousand remained. Today, conservationists estimate that there are fewer than thirty thousand of these magnificent animals living in Asia and Africa.

The five species of rhinos left in the world are all considered endangered by the United States Fish and Wildlife Service's Threatened and Endangered Species System List. This list includes plant and animal species worldwide that are threatened and endangered.

The International Union for the Conservation of Nature and Natural Resources (IUCN), also known as the World Conservation Union, is a worldwide organization made up of many groups that volunteer their services and expertise to try to save endangered species, including the rhino. The IUCN has placed the Sumatran, Javan, and black rhino species on its critically endangered list, which is known as the Red List of Threatened Species.

The concern for the dwindling number of rhinos left in the world is widespread and includes conservation organizations, private citizens, zoos, and national and state governments. While some progress has been made in protecting rhinos and introducing breeding programs to help ensure that populations will not simply vanish, it is still a race against time, poachers, and loss of habitat to save the rhino.

Rhino Horns

Rhino horns can bring up to $500,000 per pound on the black market. For centuries, the Chinese have used rhino horn in medicines because they believe that it reduces fever, among other things. Some studies done by researchers at a university in Hong Kong have shown that rhino horn does reduce fever in rats. But researchers have also found that Chinese traditional medicines containing the horns of water buffalo, which are not endangered, also work to reduce fevers. And in the 1990s, use of rhino horn powder for traditional Chinese medicine decreased greatly, along with demand for the ingredient. This was an encouraging turn of events. But in 2008 things changed.

A rumor began in Vietnam that a local politician was cured of cancer by taking rhino horn powder. Although there is no proof and traditional Chinese medicine shows no record of cancer-curing properties in rhino horn, the market demand shot up. In addition, it is being used as a party drug and a hangover cure.[1]

Rhinoceroses were brought to the brink of extinction by hunters, most of whom were seeking the horn, which is highly valued in Asian medicine.

A Plan of Action

Laws banning the trade of rhino horn seem to have had little effect. There are, however, programs sponsored by conservation organizations that are looking into substitutes for rhino horn, such as water buffalo horn.

Jambiyas, the decorative daggers prized by wealthy Yemenis, account for some use of rhino horn. Because of their rhino horn handles, they are prized and passed down for generations to young men as a symbol of masculinity. The trade in black rhino horn that is used to make dagger handles is largely responsible for the decline of the black rhino population, but things are looking up. Yemen has drastically reduced its use of the rhino horn after being encouraged to use water buffalo horn for dagger handles, as well as not allowing dagger makers to be relicensed if they were caught using rhino horn.

Education to Save Rhinos

Letting people know about the effects of the rhino horn trade on the animal's worldwide population is one way to help ensure the rhino's survival. Conservation groups and zoo programs hope to raise awareness that the world is dangerously close to losing several, if not all, rhino species. To that end, the United States Fish and Wildlife Service began a program aimed at educating Asian immigrants, who were the most likely to use traditional Chinese medicines containing rhino horn, about just how few rhinos are left in the wild.

The United States Fish and Wildlife Service, along with the Convention on International Trade in Endangered Species of Wild Fauna and Flora, or CITES, also passed the Rhinoceros and Tiger Conservation Fund of 1994. As stated in the law, its purpose is "to assist in the conservation of rhinoceros and tigers by supporting the conservation programs of nations whose activities directly or indirectly affect rhinoceros and tiger populations."[2] The law also includes resolutions that prohibit the trade of endangered wildlife species and provide money for ongoing conservation efforts.

Money talks in other ways. The government of the United States monitors countries that are involved in the illegal trade of endangered animals. If those countries do not seem to be adhering to the laws protecting the animals, they can and have been fined large amounts of money.

Dehorning Rhinos

Another attempt to halt the trade in rhino horn and save the rhino from extinction is a practice called dehorning. The thought behind this practice is that a rhino without its horn is less attractive to poachers. When a rhino is dehorned, it is first shot with a tranquilizer dart to render it unconscious. Then a veterinarian removes the horn with a saw, leaving only a stub, which will grow back at the rate of about two inches a year.

The program is not foolproof, though, and it is expensive. Unfortunately, poachers still sometimes kill dehorned animals to save themselves the trouble of tracking a rhino only to find it does not have its horn.

However, rhinos that have been dehorned in Africa in recent years have shown an almost 30 percent higher chance of survival compared to rhinos with horns.

Dehorning a rhino is one idea to help save the animals from extinction. By removing the valuable part, they hope to deter poachers.

Track the Poachers

Once a rhino is killed and its horn is removed, strategies to track the poachers and traders become important to shutting down the illegal market for horns. One way that conservationists hope to do this is through rhino horn "fingerprinting." Horns reflect the habitat of the rhino, since elements of local vegetation, climate, and geology are absorbed through digestion. Being able to identify where a particular horn came from could be a useful tool for controlling the illegal trade in rhino horn.

Another way to identify and track a rhino horn is by inserting a microchip into it. This is done while a rhino is unconscious, often when the rhino is being moved to a safer location.

Moves to Safer Ground

Translocation involves moving rhinos from wild habitats where they are easily poached to safer areas where they can be watched and protected. National parks and conservation organizations have undertaken translocation projects in both Africa and India. The rhinos are moved to Intensive Protection Zones, or IPZs. These can be on government property or in private sanctuaries. One of the most famous translocation efforts was called Operation Rhino. It started in 1961 by redistributing white rhinos and continued into the 1970s as a means of saving the black rhino from extinction.

Translocating an enormous animal such as the rhino is no easy task, but there have been breakthroughs over the years that have made the process easier. The tranquilizers used to sedate the animals have improved. Once a rhino is shot with a tranquilizer dart, it will sink to the ground. The dart is often shot from a helicopter rather than tracking the animal on the ground, which can be dangerous. Helicopters are also used to transport the rhino in a special net.

Legalizing Rhino Horn Trade

The sale of rhino horn and other rhino products has been banned in 130 countries, but the ban has not stopped poaching, as the

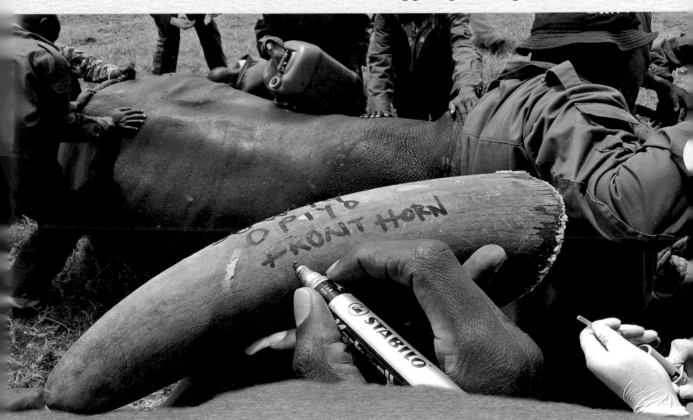

Officers from the Kenya Wildlife Services attend to a sedated black rhino. They will implant microchips in an effort to stem poaching of the endangered mammal.

value of rhino horn on the black market continues to increase. Some wildlife officials believe the way to deal with this is to lift the ban. There is a large supply of rhino horn in Africa that has been obtained through the dehorning program, and some officials feel that making those horns available legally would help end poaching. Other officials feel that if rhinos could be raised on farms, as cattle are, and then dehorned, the supply of rhino horn would satisfy the demand, and the rhino would be saved from extinction. These advocates of legalizing trade in rhino horn believe that the money from legal trade could then be used to fund programs that protect the rhino.

chapter five

Future Outlook for Rhinos

More than a decade ago, two black rhino calves were abandoned by their mothers in South Africa. Workers at a rehabilitation center cared for the young animals. After their time in the center, they were moved to the Addo Elephant National Park in the Eastern Cape. In 2004, they were successfully released back into the wild. The work at these centers is one way conservationists are trying to keep the species protected.

Of the many rhino species that once roamed the world, only five remain. Although rhinos have been around for millions of years, humans have brought them to the brink of extinction. If efforts to save these species are unsuccessful, rhinos could cease to exist in our lifetime.

Populations

The white rhino nearly became extinct at the turn of the twentieth century. Conservationists took action, though, and those animals were saved. By 1961, there were enough rhinos to translocate some as part of Operation Rhino. White rhino populations are still

Park rangers protect the rhinos and guard them from poachers.

increasing, and there are more than twenty thousand of them living in South Africa, where they are protected and breeding programs are in effect.

The black rhino has not fared as well as the white rhino. The black rhino population has dropped from about 65,000 in 1970 to about 5,055 today.[1] The black rhino has also benefited from translocation; its population in South Africa is growing because of conservation efforts there on the part of the government and private citizens.

Of the three species of Asian rhinos, the Indian rhino has the largest population. More than 3,000 live in northern India and

For the most part, rhinos avoid human beings. If threatened, however, rhinos will charge people, and mothers with calves will charge whether they are provoked or not.

southern Nepal. Poaching remains a problem, but this species is fiercely protected by Indian and Nepalese wildlife authorities.

The Javan rhino population remains unchanged at fewer than fifty for almost thirty years.[2]

The most seriously endangered rhino species, the Sumatran rhino, is actually greater in number than the Javan rhino. About one hundred exist today, but they are the most seriously threatened by humans. Like other rhino species, these hairy rhinos are poached for their horn and other body parts. Their habitat is shrinking each day as humans move farther into it.

Rhinos and the Future

There are many things being done by conservation groups to save the rhino from extinction. Captive breeding programs in zoos and rhino sanctuaries offer some hope that the rhino will not disappear from the face of the earth. The American Zoo and Aquarium Association have instituted the Species Survival Plan to encourage captive breeding programs.

Not all conservationists believe that breeding programs are the answer, however. Some consider them to be last-ditch efforts to save rhinos and point out that these programs do not address the bigger picture of protecting habitat, stopping illegal poaching and trade in rhino parts, and returning rhinos to the wild. But the question remains, how can we return rhinos to the wild without captive breeding programs?

Is there more to the story of the two rehabilitated rhinos you read about at the beginning of this chapter? One of the animals, named Thandi, was attacked by poachers in 2012. They cut off her horn, but she survived! And the story gets even better. In January 2015, Thandi added one more number to the population of black rhinos when she gave birth to a healthy calf of her own.

Wildlife veterinarian William Fowlds observed the pair from a distance, as mother rhinos do not wait for a threat to defend their calves, and confirmed that both Thandi and her baby are doing

Fast Fact!

Rhinos communicate through their poop! Their piles of dung leave messages for other rhinos. Since each rhino's smell is different, its droppings identify its owner and mark its territory. It also tells a rhino's age and gender.

A zookeeper feeds a rhino at the Sedgwick County Zoo as part of their captive breeding program.

well in the Kariega Game Reserve.[3] This story is a reminder of the people who work hard to protect the future of the rhinos, as well as the good that can come from their efforts.

Chapter Notes

Chapter 1. The Ancient Rhino

1. The International Rhino Foundation, "2013 State of the Rhino" n.d., <http://www.rhinos.org/rhinos/state-of-the-rhino-2013> (January 30, 2015).

Chapter 2. A Look at Vegetarian Giants

1. Louis and Margery Milne, *The Secret Life of Animals* (New York: Dutton, 1993), p. 177.

2. The International Rhino Foundation, "Rhino Information—White Rhino," n.d., < http://www.rhinos.org/rhinos/white-rhino> (January 30, 2015).

3. Save the Rhino, Javan Rhino Information, March 2012, <http://www.savetherhino.org/rhino_info/species_of_rhino/javan_rhinos/factfile_javan_rhino> (January 30, 2015).

4. Michael Nichols, *Keepers of the Kingdom* (New York: Thomasson-Grant & Lickle, 1996), p. 14.

5. The Cincinnati Zoo and Botanical Garden, "Cincinnati Zoo's Rhino Makes History with an Unprecedented Third Calf," *ScienceDaily,* May 3, 2007, <http://www.sciencedaily.com/releases/2007/05/070501095539.htm> (January 30, 2015).

6. Ibid.

7. Laura McVicker, "Black Rhino Born at San Diego Zoo," *NBC Universal Media,* July 18, 2014, <http://www.nbcsandiego.com/news/local/Black-Rhino-Born-at-San-Diego-Zoo-267732721.html> (January 30, 2015).

Chapter 3. The Rhino's Predator

1. Save the Rhino, "Poaching: The Statistics" n.d., <http://www.savetherhino.org/rhino_info/poaching_statistics> (January 30, 2015).

2. Tony Hare, Habitats (New York: MacMillan, 1994), p. 89.

Chapter 4. A Plan for Rhinos

1. Gwynn Guilford, "Why Does a Rhino Horn Cost $300,000? Because Vietnam Thinks It Cures Cancer and Hangovers," *Atlantic,* May 15, 2013, <http://www.theatlantic.com/business/archive/2013/05/why-does-a-rhino-horn-cost-300-000-because-vietnam-thinks-it-cures-cancer-and-hangovers/275881> (January 30, 2015).

2. United States Fish and Wildlife Service, International Affairs, "Rhinoceros and Tiger Conservation Fund," n.d., <http://www.fws.gov/international/wildlife-without-borders/rhino-and-tiger-conservation-fund.html > (January 30, 2015).

Chapter 5. Future Outlook for Rhinos

1. The International Rhino Foundation, "Rhino Information—Black Rhino," n.d., < http://www.rhinos.org/rhinos/black-rhino > (January 30, 2015).

2. Nick Eason, CNN.com, "Rare Javan Rhinos Back From the Brink," October 12, 2001, <http://www.cnn.com/2001/WORLD/asiapcf/southeast/10/12/indonesia.rhino/> (January 30, 2015).

3. Associated Press, "Rhino Attacked by Poachers Gives Birth," *Washington Post,* January 15, 2015, <http://www.washingtonpost.com/lifestyle/kidspost/rhino-attacked-by-poachers-gives-birth/2015/01/15/fa08b93c-9b85-11e4-96cc-e858eba91ced_story.html> (January 30, 2015).

Glossary

Agent Orange—An herbicide that kills the leaves of plants and was used widely during the Vietnam War.

breeding program—A plan used to reproduce animals for a few generations. The program is often used by conservationists to reproduce species that are endangered.

browser—An animal that eats the leaves from trees and bushes.

captive—Being confined or held in a safe place.

conservation—The protection of plants, animals, and natural resources.

endangered—In danger of becoming extinct and not existing on earth anymore.

extinction—The death of an entire group, or species, of living things.

grazer—An animal that eats mostly grasses.

keratin—A protein that makes up hair, nails, and horns.

poacher—A person who kills or steals wild animals illegally.

population—The total number of people, animals, or plants living in a specific area.

predator—An animal that hunts and eats other animals for food.

prehensile—Adapted to grasp or wrap around something.

species—A group of animals or plants that have similar features. They can produce offspring of the same kind.

threatened—A group of animals that is close to becoming endangered.

Further Reading

Books

Baillie, Marilyn, Jonathan Baillie, and Ellen Butcher. *How to Save a Species.* Toronto: Owlkids Books, 2014.

Borgeson, Grace. *Douwlina: A Rhino's Story.* Houston, Tex.: Bright Sky Press, 2012.

Charman, Andy. *I Wonder Why Dinosaurs Died Out and Other Questions About Extinct and Endangered Animals.* New York, N.Y.: Kingfisher, 2013.

Claus, Matteson. *Animals and Deforestation.* New York, N.Y.: Gareth Stevens Publishing, 2014.

Yolen, Jane. *Animal Stories: Heartwarming True Tales from the Animal Kingdom.* Washington, D.C.: National Geographic Children's Books, 2014.

Zane, Dory. *How to Track a Rhinoceros.* New York, N.Y.: Windmill Books, 2014.

Web Sites

fws.gov/international/animals/rhinos.html
U.S. Fish and Wildlife Service's information about rhinos.

savetherhino.org/rhino_info/species_of_rhino
Learn more about the five species of rhinos.

worldwildlife.org/species/rhino
Wealth of information on endangered and threatened animals.

Index